COSTA RICA

AN EXPAT'S TRAVEL GUIDE TO MOVING

& LIVING IN COSTA RICA

MELISSA NICOLE JOHNSON

Copyright ©2016 by Inspired Word Publishers. All rights reserved.

Inspired Word Publishers

PO BOX 1933

Carrollton, GA 30112-0036

Printed in the United States of America

No part of this book may be reproduced in any written, electronic, recording, or photocopying without written permission of the publisher or author.

ISBN-13: 978-0692712207

ISBN-10: 0692712208

Why I Wrote This Book

For a variety of reasons, there are an increasing number of expats who want to move to a foreign country. Some of the reasons for wanting to relocate include a desire for a more relaxed lifestyle, year-round warm climate, mesmerizing views of nature…long sandy beaches, crystal-clear lakes, waterfalls, streams, towering volcanoes, lush green valleys, and mesmerizing waterfalls. Others are looking for a lower cost of living, a safe retirement haven, affordable healthcare, stable democracy, and cultural exposure. If you are seeking these amenities a logical choice is Costa Rica. Indeed, Costa Rica has something for everyone and has been endorsed by *International Living* as an overseas destination since the 1980s.

However, moving can be difficult – even to Costa Rica, and there is always that family member, friend, book, blog, newsletter, or magazine spreading fear and to discourage you from pursuing your dream – moving to someplace exotic. Most of the problems that occur during a move come from lack of preparation and poor information. Unfortunately, many times there is little information available about the place you want to move to or the information available isn't exhaustive enough to be a valuable resource for anyone who wants to embark on this life-changing move. This compounds the difficulties of moving.

What if you had a resource that could easily explain the steps you should take, what you should look out for, what you should expect, were you can get information, and how to avoid the common mistakes and pitfalls that plagues most travelers?

This is precisely what Costa Rica: *An Expat's Travel Guide to Living & Moving in Costa Rica* will help you achieve. My desire is to provide you, an expat who wants to move and live in Costa Rica, with an A to Z knowledge about the entire process so that your move is as pleasurable and easy as possible.

WHY YOU SHOULD READ THIS BOOK

This book will help you get started on your life-changing journey of moving and living in Costa Rica. From exploring the beautiful beaches and landscapes to exploring some of the setbacks that you might encounter; this book will give you a truthful account and precise details about the experience of moving and living in Costa Rica.

Costa Rica: An Expat's Travel Guide to Moving and Living in Costa Rica aims at sharing the knowledge you need to get you started on your move to Costa Rica. From visa information, booking flights, giving you an insight on where to stay in Costa Rica, how to get around, exploring the country's rich culture, nightlife/entertainment scene and cuisine, saving money; you will get an in depth insight about it all from this one simple book.

Other books lack specific detail, are difficult to read, too long, expensive, and plain out boring. Not this one!

This book is fun, informative, easy to read, and full of pertinent information to make your dream of living in Costa Rica a reality and a pleasant experience.

Table Of Contents

Chapter 1. An Introduction To Costa Rica
- Location
- Geography
- Government
- Traveling to Costa Rica
- Economy
- Education
- Healthcare
- Religion
- Languages

Chapter 2. Visa Information
- How to Get a Visa
- Preparing for Embassy Interviews
- Flight/Airport Information
- How to Get Great Deals on Flights
- Required Documents For Entry
- Travelers Bringing Pets

Chapter 3. Welcome to Costa Rica
- Where to Stay
- Hotels/Hostels
- Apartments
- How to Save on Housing Costs

Chapter 4. How to Get around Costa Rica
- Available Modes of Transport
- Road Transport

    Domestic Flights

    How to Save on Travel Costs

Chapter 5. The Costa Rican Culture

    The People

    Cultural Practices

    Cuisine

    How to Save Money on Food in Costa Rica

Chapter 6. What to do In Costa Rica

    Costa Rica's Attractions

    Entertainment in Costa Rica

    Nightlife in Costa Rica

    How to Save Money When Sightseeing in Costa Rica

Chapter 7. Making Money in Costa Rica

    How to Get a job in Costa Rica

    Available Work Opportunities in Costa Rica

    Salaries/Wages

    Volunteering in Costa Rica

Chapter 8. Education in Costa Rica

    The School System

    Paying for School

    Spanish Language Schools in Costa Rica

Chapter 9. Shipping and Mail Service in Costa Rica

    Mail

    Modes of Shipping

    Other Methods to Bring Items to Costa Rica

    How to Save on Shipping Costs

Chapter 10. Getting Married in Costa Rica

Marriage Laws in Costa Rica

Wedding Venues in Costa Rica

Planning a Wedding in Costa Rica

How to Save on Wedding Costs in Costa Rica

About the Author

Other Books Featured by Inspired Word Publishers

One Last Thing

Chapter 1

AN INTRODUCTION TO COSTA RICA

When you think about Costa Rica what comes to mind? Probably imagery of tropical sandy beaches, crystal-clear lakes, crashing waterfalls, and towering waterfalls comes to mind. Well, you aren't entirely wrong, but there is much more to Costa Rica than its beautiful landscape, beautiful people and rich culture. Costa Rica is a well-rounded country that will transform your life-changing move into a dream come true.

LOCATION

Costa Rica is located in a region called Central America, which occupies the southernmost portion of the North America continent.

You might wonder why it is important to know where exactly Costa Rica is located. The reality is that few people bother with the location of any place they visit and even fewer people can find different places on a map, not even their own country! Moving to Costa Rica will literally mean changing your location, not only by a couple of miles, but for possibly thousands of miles away.

It also makes you look good to be able to talk about the country's location to friends and family when telling them about your big move. Prepare yourself for the resounding question that most people will ask, 'Where is Costa Rica located?'

GEOGRAPHY

With a population of about 4.7 million people, Costa Rica is quite a small country. Costa Rica actually means 'Rich Coast' in English and is divided into 7 provinces, providing an extensive beautiful region to explore.

The 7 Costa Rican provinces include: San Jose, with a population of 1.4 million; Limon, with a population of 386,862; Alajuela, with a population of 846,146; Puntarenas, with a population of 410,929; Heredia, with a population of 433,677; Guanacaste, with a population of 326,953; and Cartago, with a population of 490,903. The country is further divided into 81 cantons and 473 districts. San Jose, nicknamed *Chepe*, is the capital of the country. The country of Nicaragua borders the country to the north and Panama borders the country to the south.

The Costa Rican coastline stretches 801 miles (1,290 km), and the country has coastlines both on the Pacific Ocean and the Caribbean Sea.

We can't talk about the geography of Costa Rica and not mention floods, volcanoes and earthquakes. Going through these natural calamities historically shaped the country's landscape, marked by rugged mountains separating the expansive coastal plain.

Get ready for temperature soars, because the country enjoys tropical as well as subtropical climates through most of the year. The rainy season starts in May and goes on through to November and the dry season runs from December through to April. The country is said to generally experience 27 weather patterns. Areas at the beach experience the warmest temperatures going up to 90+ Fahrenheit (or 32+ Celsius) with high humidity. You can easily get around this with good air conditioning, but this could rack up a $400 monthly bill to cool your home or apartment. The country's Central Valley experiences temperate climate going up to 78 - 80 Fahrenheit and with less humidity. The mountain regions experience cooler temperatures with daytime temperatures in the 70s and night temperatures going down to around 50 to 60 degrees Fahrenheit. The mountain regions also tend to be cloudy with higher humidity and high possibility of rains.

Favorably, with raised awareness about global warming as well as devastations that affect natural resources, 27% of the country's rainforests and primary as well as secondary forests is protected by SINAC (the National System of Conservation) which oversees all the country's protected areas.

GOVERNMENT

Costa Rica is a democratic republic with Executive Power held by the president and the president's cabinet. The president is also the head of government and head of state. The Legislative Assembly, made up of 57 deputies, hold the Legislative power.

Favorably, the country's political stability attracts foreign investors as several global high-tech corporations have already started developing in the area. The government has put in place measures to prevent foreign investors from exploiting what is perceived as a "cheap" Costa Rican workforce. Foreign investors are required to hire Costa Rican citizens as their workforce.

ECONOMY

Costa Rica's main exports are poultry, beef, dairy, bananas, melons, pineapples, corn, sugar, beans, rice, coffee and timber. The primary industries in the country include medical equipment, plastic products, food processing, fertilizer, textiles and clothing and construction materials. As of 2015, Costa Rica's Gross Domestic Product was valued at $69.5 billion.

Industry globalization is happening rapidly and is one of the challenges the country is facing. The pressure to conform to free-market economies like other progressive nations has created split ideologies.

EDUCATION

In 1949 the government abolished the army, which eliminated the costs of sustaining military forces. These funds were redirected towards education and public healthcare. It is said that the "army" has been replaced with an army of teachers. The literacy rate is 95%, the highest in Latin America. The country boasts of having 6,147 institutions that provide formal education, which provides an educated workforce suitable for business. Public education is guaranteed by the country's constitution and primary education is mandatory; both preschool and high school are free. There are few state and private universities available after the 12th grade; however, the University of Costa Rica, located in the province of San Jose, is the oldest, largest, and most prestigious institution of higher learning in the country.

HEALTHCARE

When it comes to healthcare, Costa Rica provides the best healthcare services in the whole of Central America and is one of the many Latin American countries that have become popular destinations for medical tourism. Because of its low costs and excellent service, hundreds of thousands of foreigners come to Costa Rica for medical treatment each year.

The Ministry of Health and Social Security System offer free healthcare to citizens. Approximately 90% of the citizens receive public healthcare coverage. Primary healthcare facilities in Costa Rica include health clinics, with a general practitioner, nurse, clerk, pharmacist, and primary health technician. There are private clinics/hospitals which require payment in either cash/check or insurance form. Costa Rica also boasts of having a doctor to patient ratio similar to the United States.

RELIGION

The majority of Costa Ricans are Catholics and it is the predominant religion in the country with 76.3% of the population practicing the faith. Evangelicals protestants represent 13.7% of the population. Jehovah's Witnesses represent 1.3% of the population, 4.8% practice other faiths including Hinduism and Islam, 0.7% practices other protestant faiths, and 3.2% of the population is not religious.

LANGUAGES

Spanish is the primary language spoken by most people. Although it is not necessary to know Spanish if you are visiting as a tourist, if you do intend to move to Costa Rica it is very important for you to learn Spanish. Actually, if you finally get permanent residency being able to communicate fluently in Spanish is almost always a prerequisite to getting a job in the country. However, English is also vastly spoken in the country.

TRAVELING TO COSTA RICA

Getting a flight is the easiest way to get to Costa Rica. The country has two international airports; Juan Santamaria Airport (SJO) and Daniel Oduber Airport (LIR). SJO is located within the Central Valley region near San Jose while LIR, located in Liberia, facilitates access to destinations in the northwestern Guanacaste region. There are few direct flights from Europe and the rest of the world going into Costa Rica. The majority of flights pass through the United States, which means that if you are from a foreign country you should make sure that you comply with entry requirements to the United States.

Look up South American airlines such as LAN and Taca, because they often have great deals on flights.

Chapter 2

VISA INFORMATION

If you are an American, you will be happy to know that you won't need a visa to travel to Costa Rica. However, entry requirements will vary depending on your nationality and where you are flying from.

HOW TO GET A VISA

It is important to take some time and gather as much information as possible about getting a visa to Costa Rica. Again, this varies depending on your nationality and the country that you are applying for the visa from. This is very important in order to know how long you can legally stay within the country and to familiarize yourself with the country's immigration rules and regulations.

Generally, a valid passport will grant you entry into Costa Rica. The following outlines entry requirements to Costa Rica depending on the countries of origin:

- **Group One**

If you are from the countries listed below a valid passport will grant you entry into Costa Rica and a 90-day stay without a visa.

Africa	South Africa
Asia	Israel, Japan, Singapore, South Korea
Caribbean	Bahamas, Barbados, Trinidad and Tobago
Central America	Panama
Europe	Andorra, Austria, Belgium, Bulgaria, Croatia, Cyprus, Czech Republic, Denmark, Estonia, Finland, France, Germany, Greece, Ireland,

	Italy, Latvia, Liechtenstein, Lithuania, Luxemburg, Malta, Monaco, Montenegro, Netherlands, Norway, Poland, Portugal, , Romania, San Marino, Serbia, Slovakia, Slovenia, Spain, Sweden, Switzerland, United Kingdom, Vatican
Micronesia and Polynesia	Australia, New Zealand
North America	United States of America, Canada, Mexico, Puerto Rico
South America	Argentina, Brazil, Chile, Paraguay, Uruguay

Be sure to know precisely where you will be staying, for how long, and have your custom forms filled out when you get to immigration.

- **Group Two**

If you are from the countries listed below a valid passport will grant you entry into Costa Rica for a 30-day stay without a visa.

Africa	Mauritius, São Tomé and Principe, Seychelles
Asia	Maldives, Philippines, Turkey,
Central America and the Antilles	Antigua and Barbuda, Belize, El Salvador, Guatemala, Honduras, Saint Kits and Nevis, Santa Lucia
Micronesia and Polynesia	Fiji, Micronesia, Kiribati, Marshall Islands, Nauru, Palau, Samoa, Solomon Islands, Tonga, Tuvalu, Vanuatu

South America	Bolivia, Grenada, Guyana, Venezuela, Surinam, Saint Vincent and the Grenadines

As well as the 15 islands that fall under the Northern Mariana Islands areas.

If you fall in this group you will be able to seek an extension while inside the country.

- **Group Three**

If you are from the countries listed below a valid passport and a consular visa will allow you entry and a 30-day stay in Costa Rica.

Africa	Algeria, Angola, Benin, Burkina Faso, Botswana, Burundi, Cameroon, Cape Verde, Central African Republic, Chad, Comoros, The Republic of Congo, Djibouti, Egypt, Equatorial Guinea, Gabon, Gambia, Ghana, Guinea Bissau, Ivory Coast, Kenya. Lesotho, Liberia, Libya, Mali, Malawi, Mauritania, Morocco, Mozambique, Namibia, Niger, Nigeria, Rwanda, Swaziland, Senegal, Sierra Leone, Sudan, Tanzania, Togo, Tunisia, Uganda, Zambia
Asia	Bahrain, Bhutan, Brunei, Cambodia, India, Indonesia, Jordan, Kazakhstan, Kyrgyzstan, Kuwait, Lebanon, Laos, Malaysia, Mongolia, Nepal, Oman, Pakistan, Qatar, Saudi Arabia, Timor-Leste, Taiwan, Tajikistan, Thailand, Turkmenistan, United Arab Emirates, Uzbekistan, Vietnam, Yemen,

Central America and the Antilles	Dominican Republic, Nicaragua
Europe	Albania, Armenia, Azerbaijan, Belarus, Bosnia and Herzegovina, Georgia, Kosovo, Macedonia, Moldova, Russia, Ukraine,
South America	Columbia, Peru

Countries that fall under the Sahrawi Arab Republic territory also fall under this category

- **Group Four**

If you are from the countries listed below a valid passport and a restricted visa will allow you entry and a 30-day stay in Costa Rica.

Africa	Eritrea, Ethiopia
Asia	Afghanistan, Bangladesh, China, North Korea, Palestine, Syria
Caribbean	Cuba, Haiti, Jamaica

PREPARING FOR EMBASSY INTERVIEWS

Once again, this will be dependent on your country of origin as well as the country from which you will be entering Costa Rica. As outlined above, you might not need a visa to enter Costa Rica or you might need a consular or restricted visa.

Your passport should be valid and have at least 6 months on it before expiration. A return ticket is also a requirement as well as having $100 cash for every month that you plan to stay in the country.

FLIGHT/AIRPORT INFORMATION

You can lookup flight information yourself or you may choose to enlist the services of a travel agent. However, looking for flights yourself will give you more flexibility to weigh your options and choose the best deal.

HOW TO GET GREAT DEALS ON FLIGHTS

The costs of flights to Costa Rica, just like pretty much anywhere else in the world, is dependent on the time of year. Expect to pay high flight costs in December, January, August and July. Summer (May to November) is the best months to travel to Costa Rica if you are looking for great deals on flights. However, when traveling from Europe or the U.S. to Costa Rica in December going into mid-June flights might be more affordable. Traveling on weekends tends to be more costly compared to traveling during weekdays.

Something to also note is that when traveling from Costa Rica to any other country you will have to pay a departure tax of about $29. This is not included in your air ticket cost and is payable at the airport in the local currency colones (CRC), dollars, by cash or credit card. Starting in December 2014 this charge was to be included in flight ticket costs. It is important to check whether your ticket indicates that you have paid this cost. If it doesn't, simply pay as outlined above.

REQUIRED DOCUMENTS FOR ENTRY

Once you arrive in Costa Rica you will be directed to immigration. You will be required to present documentation including your passport and any other relevant documentation. The immigration process takes anywhere from 10 minutes to an hour or more, depending on general traffic at the airport on that particular day.

After immigration, your next stop will be to baggage claim and you should expect to wait about 10 to 20 minutes for your luggage. The next stop from here will be customs. Be very careful with items you choose to take with you. Any item that is considered a weapon will be disallowed and this includes nail clippers. Also, lotions that have high contents of alcohol and body sprays have been known to be confiscated before carry on bags go through luggage scanners. Once you pass through customs you will then leave the airport.

TRAVELORS BRINGING PETS

If you chose to bring your cat or dog with you to Costa Rica you will need to obtain an endorsed health certificate issued by a licensed veterinarian. The health examination should be conducted 2 weeks before the departure date. Dogs should be vaccinated against distemper, hepatitis, leptospirosis, and rabies. Cats should be vaccinated for rabies. On your return trip, if leaving, you will need a Certificate of Good Health for your pet(s) from a veterinarian in Costa Rica.

Chapter 3

WELCOME TO COSTA RICA

The day is here, you have finally moved to Costa Rica but are you prepared to start your life in the tropical country? Putting a roof over your head will be one of the first priorities you have towards starting your Costa Rican life.

To start off, Costa Rica offers different types of legal <u>temporary</u> residencies including:

- "*Pensionado*" applies to any person who is retired from his/her usual occupation and who is already receiving pension benefits.

    <u>Married Couple *Pensionado* Income:</u> A married couple needs to show proof of only one monthly pension, of at least $1,000 per month, for both husband and wife to qualify for residency. The pension recipient can be either spouse.

    <u>Income Requirement:</u> Must show proof of monthly income from a qualified pension plan of at least $1,000 per month.

    A pension plan can include amongst others: local, state/provincial and Federal government pensions from most countries. Canadian Old Age Pension System, U.S. Social Security Administration and Railroad Retirement benefits, private pension plans, 401K plans, school district pension, IRA/Keogh distributions, etc. To be a qualified pension plan, the pension must be payable to the resident applicant "for life." It also refers to a person who holds a lifetime annuity of $1,000 or more monthly guaranteeing them a steady source of income. This is commonly the type of residency obtained by older adults, but it doesn't have an age restriction.

Currency Exchange Requirement: Once approved, the resident agrees to exchange a minimum of $1,000 per month (or $12,000 per year) into Costa Rican currency (colones) at the official dollar-colon rate in effect at the time of the exchange.

In-Country Requirement: Once approved, the resident agrees to live in Costa Rica for at least one (1) day per year.

Type of Residency: Temporary. The resident can apply for permanent residency after being a temporary resident for 3 years.

Work Permit: None issued until the resident becomes a permanent resident.

- *"Rentista"* applies to individuals who (1) are not yet retired, (2) do not need to work while living in Costa Rica, (3) are receiving guaranteed, unearned income from investments or other sources, and (4) who can prove that the non-earned income is guaranteed to be received for at least 24 months (2 years). However, most foreigners obtain this residency status by means of a notarized letter from a bank or financial institution indicating that the applicant has on deposit at least $60,000 to be paid out at a monthly rate of $2,500 for a period of 24 months. It is not mandatory that the bank account be held in Costa Rica; however, it is easier to obtain the required bank letter when the account is held in a Costa Rican bank. Once this period lapses you will be required to bank another $60,000.

Income Requirement: Applicant must prove his/her ability to receive $2,500 per month of unearned income for 24 months (2 years). Other sources of income include savings, interest or dividends.

Married Couple *Rentista* Income: The exact same $2,500 per month income requirement applies to a single, or to married applicants, or to applicants with dependent children.

Currency Exchange Requirement: Once approved, the resident agrees to exchange a minimum of $2,500 per month (or $30,000 per year) into Costa Rican currency (colones) at the official dollar-colon rate in effect at the time of the exchange.

In-Country Requirement: Once approved, the resident agrees to live in Costa Rica for at least one (1) day per year.

Type of Residency: Temporary. The resident can apply for permanent residency after being a temporary resident for 3 years.

Work Permit: None issued until the resident becomes a permanent resident.

- Those on international missions or government assignments may also be granted residency.

- A "representante", applies to someone who is the CEO of a Costa Rican business, may also be granted residency albeit with restrictions.

- An investor, an individual who makes a direct investment in Costa Rica, can also get legal residency provided they invest at least $200,000.

- Permanent residency is granted to a qualifying person who is a first-degree relative (spouse, father, mother, brother, sister) of a Costa Rica citizen or to any other person who has held another legal form of residency (i.e. rentista) for a period of three years. Also, permanent residency can be obtained after staying in the country for more than 3 years through legal residency as outlined above. Just like temporary residency, permanent residency must also be regularly renewed. A permanent resident can work and run/own a company in the country receiving an income through it.

It is possible to go through the residency process on your own and skip the legal fees. Doing it on your own costs around $300 and includes filing fees, payments to translators and lawyers, per person. However, this plan of action is not advised. It is highly recommended that you obtain a reputable lawyer to guide you through the process. Don't settle for the cheaper non-lawyer "fixers" and their false promises. Cheaper is not always better. There are numerous cases where people have gotten in trouble with immigration trying to save $100. The cost of hiring a lawyer should cost between $600 to $2,000 per person. This may sound expensive, but a lawyer will make sure that you have completed and signed all the right documents, will take you to the right government office, and ensure that you submit your documents to the right person. An extra bonus of having a lawyer is that your waiting time is reduced at the immigration office where long sprawling lines are common. Lawyers have a special window at the immigration office with no wait.

Citizenship is granted after living in the country as a legal resident for an accumulated period of 7 years. You may apply for citizenship if you are married to a Costa Rican resident and have lived in the country for 2 years. If you are from certain countries, such as Latin American countries and Spain, you may apply for citizenship after living in Costa Rica for 5 years. It is important to know that it takes about 1 to 2 years to obtain citizenship after applying.

It is important to know that some of the key documents required for all residency applications in Costa Rica will include:

- A letter addressed to the head of immigration with the reasons you are applying for residency.

- A Certificate of Good Conduct (from a police department), which is valid for at least 6 months, obtained from your country or origin/residence. You will need one as well as your spouse (if applicable) and children who are between the ages of 15 to 25.

- Certificate of registration with home embassy.

- Marriage certificate or divorce certificate (if applicable)

- Birth certificate of all applicants (yours, your spouse and children).

- *Pensionados* and *Rentistas* will also need to submit income certificates, which are valid for at least 6 months.

Dual citizenship is permitted for nationals from certain countries such as Canada and the U.S. However, with the exception of gaining citizenship through marriage to a Costa Rican national you technically may have to renounce your U.S. or Canadian citizenship.

WHERE TO STAY

You should have a general idea about where you will be staying before you get to Costa Rica, particularly if you will be staying for longer than a month. Besides knowing the specific province or city and address, the most important part about finding suitable accommodations in Costa Rica is knowing what options are available.

Some of the things to consider when looking for a place to stay include your length of stay, the quality of life you expect to have in Costa Rica, and of course - the size of your budget. Generally, a monthly budget of $1,500 will enable two people to live a comfortable life including paying for housing, utilities, food, entertainment, health insurance, with a little left over for savings. In due time, other aspects such as the proximity to your work place, transport access, and proximity to schools will determine your choice of accommodation in the country.

One general aspect you should know about housing is that it tends to be costlier in the capital city of San Jose. However, the cost of housing becomes cheaper as you move away from the capital to the country's smaller cities.

Motorcycle drivers often deliver utility bills to your doorstep. Be sure to always check out for them, because they will be stuck at the gate/fence and in unfortunate cases the wind might blow them off. Utility payments are made at the bank. Accord your utility bill payments priority or you may find your phone, electric or water supply turned off.

Personal checks are seldom used and that is why payments are frequently made at the bank. Be prepared to queue at the bank, something most people particularly from the US might not be accustomed to. The banks are where your ability to speak Spanish will be tested. There are banks that offer online bill payment services such as the state *Banco Nacional*, but most tend to be in Spanish. Remember online security measures when transacting online. Do not connect to your bank account or perform online banking activity at an Internet café, via a wireless connection using your laptop or iPad device. Another way to make utility payments is to go to the utility company and pay by cash. However, you will still have to deal with the dreaded long lines referred to as *filas*.

HOTELS/HOSTELS

More than likely, when you arrive in Costa Rica your first choice of accommodation will be a hotel. This isn't entirely a bad thing, because the country's smaller hotels provide the homely, cozy laid-back atmosphere you can enjoy as you settle into your new environment.

Hostels offer dorm type accommodation and they are your best bet for affordable housing. Hostel dorm beds cost anywhere from $8 to $20 per night. There are private hostels that are a bit costlier and go for about $30 per night. Hostels can be easily located through online city specific guides as well as sites such as MercadoLibre and Airbnb.

Most hotels in Costa Rica are family-run and generally offer a more hospitable and charming service than what is seen at the larger hotels. The country's major metropolises offer diverse hotels to meet the equally diverse needs of their guests. If you want to get immersed into the Costa Rican lifestyle and experience the country's rich traditions then staying in a small hotel is highly recommended. Hotels go for about $40 per night including bed and breakfast.

Eco-hotels, which are designed to conserve the environment, are also available in Costa Rica. This is where you want to stay if you want to be in tune with nature. They are often found in the smaller towns. They tend to be costly but if you can afford it imagine staying along the beachside or at the edge of one of Costa Rica's tropical rain forests; you will find the right eco-hotel to meet your needs in Costa Rica. There are affordable eco-hotels such as the Finca Luna Nueva Lodge, located in San Ramon, which costs $57 per night for a double room on bed and breakfast including a farm tour. Others go for $60 and upwards.

APARTMENTS
If you are staying in Costa Rica for a long period of time then renting an apartment will prove to be cheaper in the long run. You could opt for vacation rentals, which provide full-serviced or half-serviced options. However, if you are truly looking to settling down in the country then getting an apartment is your best option.

Finding an apartment in Costa Rica is a pretty much similar to just about anywhere else in the world. There are online listings, including craigslist, where you can scour through to find an apartment. Just like with hotels, the further you move away from the capital San Jose the cheaper it is to rent apartments. Generally, to rent a decent apartment will cost you around $1,200 per month and it is not unheard of to rent apartments for less than $900 in the smaller cities inclusive of all amenities. Obviously, this will depend on the size of the apartment and the amenities offered.

In summary, if you intend on staying in Costa Rica for longer than 90 days you must establish and qualify for legal residency. Look into immigration and residency laws to know how to go about it the right way. Costa Rica is generally very welcoming to new residents as long as you can show proof of sufficient financial resources, meaning you can adequately afford your stay in the country. Refer back to the types of legal residencies offered in Costa Rica.

Once again the rule of thumb is that accommodation gets cheaper the further away you are from the capital San Jose. Property by the beach also tends to be quite costly and with the high heat expect to rack up quite the bill on electricity/air conditioning.

HOW TO SAVE ON HOUSING COSTS

The best way to lower housing expense is to find a hotel/apartment in the smaller cities outside of San Jose, but you won't find them on the rental listings. This will depend on what you expect from your Costa Rican experience and generally the smaller cities will serve you well. This is why the first few weeks or months should be spent exploring the beautiful country and its cities, and who knows you might just stumble across a gem that ends up being your next new home.

Another way to lower housing expense is to get a roommate. It is possible to find American nationals or nationals from your native country offering room rentals in Costa Rica. These listings can be found from the diverse online expat sites such as Internations.org. This will again depend on your expectations. If you're looking to settle down with your family or start a new family in Costa Rica then finding a roommate probably won't interest you.

Chapter 4

HOW TO GET AROUND COSTA RICA

Costa Rica provides a host of fun and interesting activities to do and sights to see. You will need to establish a comfortable and reliable mode of transportation to explore the beautiful country. Knowing the best options available will help you lower your travel expense.

AVAILAVLE MODES OF TRANSPORT

Costa Rica offers diverse modes of transportation. There are buses, car hire services/ car rentals, taxis, and flights available to get around Costa Rica. Transportation in Costa Rica is generally affordable and it's up to you to decide what works best for your needs.

ROAD TRANSPORT

1. **Buses**

   Buses are the cheapest form of travel in Costa Rica. San Jose hosts practically all of the country's bus services. Bus fares for mid distances to long distances cost about $4 to $13.

   Goflito is one of the popular bus services, which requires booking in advance and tickets are issued with specific travel dates as well as seat numbers. It is possible to travel without making reservations, but to be on the safe side with such transport services, always book your tickets in advance. Also, with advance bookings, make sure that the travel dates indicated on your ticket are correct. You won't get refunds or change tickets in such cases, even if the mistake wasn't yours. It is also not possible to buy roundtrip tickets and you should make sure to buy a return ticket once you get to your destination to avoid disappointments.

The *Ticabuses* buses are the most comfortable with good seats, sufficient legroom, good luggage space and air-conditioning.

Costa Rican bus schedules are known to change frequently and it is important to keep track of their schedules.

2. **Car**

    If you want control over how you get around in Costa Rica renting a car will serve you well. You can also choose to buy a car. However, you should know that driving in Costa Rica isn't cheap. This is because you will have to cover insurance costs, vehicle inspection costs, registration, and of course maintenance costs.

    It is important to find out if you need an international driver's license to drive in Costa Rica, but if you are from the UK, US and Canada a valid driver's license will enable you to drive in the country.

    The speed limit is often marked on road surfaces and signs. The typical speeding limit for driving on the highway is between 75kph to 90kph. In construction zones the speed limit reduces to 25kph to 40kph. Traffic offences will get you hefty fines referred to as *multas* and they include driving without wearing your seatbelt, driving through a red light, or using your cell phone while driving. These traffic offences can get you a $400 fine or more. Speeding fines are common and if you are caught speeding get ready to pay up to a $575 fine.

    Marchamo is a type of vehicle registration fee. Costa Rica requires all vehicles to carry the proof of circulation in the form of a sticker displayed on your windshield. All vehicles in Costa Rica pay this type of road tax and it is charged by the

INS, the local insurance company that is owned by the government. Marchamo is renewable from November 1st to December 31st annually. Your car may be impounded if you don't have the right of circulation or sticker displayed on your windshield after January 1st. The policy can be obtained from private or public banks as well as from MOPT offices. The cost varies depending on the type of car you drive and could be anywhere from $200 to $1,000. You can find out the specific cost by going to the INS website. Also, you won't be able to obtain Marchamo if your vehicle has outstanding traffic or parking tickets.

Auto insurance is not mandatory, but every vehicle owner knows the importance of having it. Generally, an auto insurance policy that covers liability, theft and collision costs about $1,500 per year. Of course, this depends on the usual factors including the type and make of your car, its value and overall condition.

3. **Motorcycles and Bicycles**

You will need a motorcycle license to drive a motorbike around Costa Rica. A motorbike is one of the most convenient and easiest ways to get around. You can rent a small motorbike for about $70 in the smaller beach towns.

The Costa Rican terrain was built for cycling, and if you enjoy cycling you will find it a convenient way of getting around. If you are brave enough to get on the roads, be prepared to dodge potholes, other motorists and occasionally cattle.

4. **Taxis**

Taxis in Costa Rica have meters known as *marias*, which taxi drivers are legally required to use. However, it is common to find taxis that don't use meters, particularly in San Jose, and fares are agreed in advance through bargaining.

Colectovos are taxis that can be used by several passengers and drivers often charge about $0.50 from one point to another. They are less common, but are a highly economical form of transportation.

DOMESTIC FLIGHTS

For long distance travel within Costa Rica you can opt for domestic flights. Costa Rica has two domestic flight services; Nature Air and Sansa. They are reasonably economical offering flights from San Jose to the country's bordering beach towns.

Reserving your flight is recommended, but you won't be guaranteed a seat until you actually pay for the flight. Also worth noting is that the Tambor, Arenal and Quepos airports charge departure and arrival taxes of about $2 to $7.

Air Charters are available, although they can be expensive, they can also prove to be a cheaper option for traveling longer distances within Costa Rica. Most charters cost about $890 for a 7-person flight, and if the cost is split amongst the passengers it can be an economical option.

HOW TO SAVE ON TRAVEL COSTS

To save on travel costs it pays to make advance reservations. However, it is important to make the reservation and payment to guarantee a seat on buses/flights. Also, traveling on weekdays or low seasons tends to be cheaper compared to traveling during weekends.

Hitchhiking can also save you some money, but caution is highly advised. Only choose to hitchhike if you are with a companion and know precisely where you are going. Women traveling alone are discouraged from hitchhiking. Hitchhiking is particularly common on rural roads where frequent bus services are unavailable. Costa Rican nationals are generous by nature, but you should always offer to pay by asking *'Cuánto le debo?'* meaning how much do I owe?

CHAPTER 5

THE COSTA RICAN CULTURE

Costa Ricans have a vibrant culture, which they are proud of, that is celebrated often. If you have not done so already, you will learn to love the people and food in general, but it is possible to suffer from a culture shock. However, as long as you are mentally prepared to embrace a new lifestyle and immerse yourself into the Costa Rican culture you will adjust just fine.

THE PEOPLE

Costa Ricans can be the friendliest people you will ever meet and they are very welcoming to visitors. Not to say that there are no exceptions; it is possible to have a few misunderstandings here and there as would typically be expected with any frequent human interactions.

The Costa Rican people are dubbed *Ticos*, with women generally referred to as *Tica* and the men *Tico*. This stems from their tendency to 'add a little something' to words. For instance, Ticos call their grandmothers *abuela*, but with a little added something most say it as *abuelita*.

The Costa Rican people are a mixture of diverse races with 4 million of the country's population being descendants of Spanish immigrants. Many others are descendants of Europe, Central America, Asia and Africa. The Central Valley hosts most of the 'fair-skinned' Costa Ricans while the outlying regions is where *mestizos* (people of mixed ancestry mostly indigenous blood and European blood) are found. Dark skinned Ticos of Nicaraguan decent are found in the Guanacaste Province. The Caribbean coast near Limón is where you will find Costa Ricans with African lineage. The

Talamanca Mountain is where various tribes of pureblood Indians live.

Now they may look and speak differently than you, but Ticos generally share the same aspirations and fears that you may have. They are a people who work hard, want to educate their children, don't like corrupt politicians and they want to feel secure in their own country. They are also very polite to the extent that it could rub you the wrong way. This happens more if you are more straightforward and direct. Ticos seem to have a fear of appearing rude and may agree to something (in the case of contractors performing work) or promise to deliver when they can't. Be patient and take the time to understand the people and their culture.

CULTURAL PRACTICES

Ticos are all about music, dancing and family, and to some extent drinking, and who doesn't enjoy the occasional drink? They also like their music loud and you'll definitely know if there is a party around the block.

Catholic churches are often found in the central plaza, which all Costa Rican towns have. In rural villages their squares are grass fields that also double up as soccer fields. In fact, you will find soccer fields in front of most churches in Costa Rica, because soccer is quite a big deal in the country as well. An interesting occurrence is that Catholicism coexists with Costa Rican supernatural beliefs like spells and spirits.

March 19th the country's towns celebrate the day of San Jose. On August 2nd, the country honors their patron Saint La Negrita. On August 30th, the country celebrates the day of San Ramon and on May 15th the country celebrates the day of San Ididro Labrado.

The Guanacaste region is where you will find *Topes* and *Fiestas*. *Topes,* referring to rodeos, are popular in the region as well as in small towns all around the country. The rodeos are common in summer (February/April) and they offer a variety of activities. These include milking and herding competitions, Bull Riding shows, horse maneuvering, bull fighting and calf-roping competitions. Cattle farming is predominantly practiced in the region and every ranch has its own standard rituals.

CUISINE

Costa Rican cuisine is savory, hearty and never disappoints. Expect generous portions served and freshly brewed coffee as well as colorful fruits at every meal.

Costa Ricans love fresh bread and it is almost a ritual to visit the bakery every morning to purchase some freshly baked bread. The same goes to fruits and vegetables, weekly trips to the farmer's market for fresh vegetables, fruits and produce are customary in Costa Rica.

Rice and beans are Costa Rica's staples and they are featured in almost every meal including maize meal in the form of tortillas. Costa Rican meals also feature chicken, pork rinds, eggs, beef joints and chorizo which are several types of pork sausages.

Gallo Pinto is what Costa Ricans refer to as breakfast and it often consists of leftovers from dinner including the staple rice and beans, bell peppers and onions served with scrambled eggs, fried plantains and *quesco fresco* which is fresh cheese.

Casado is lunch comprising yet again the staple rice and beans accompanied by pork chops, fried chicken, stewed beef or tilapia. Sides often include spaghetti, fried plantains known as *patacones*, stewed squash known as *picadillo* and fresh cassava.

Dinner will comprise rice and beans, but it could simply be a meal of rice and chicken. French fries served with pink sauce made from mayo and ketchup (*salas rosada*) may also be served for dinner.

There are savory variations of rice and beans served with coconut milk, providing quite the treat.

Fresh sea bass is used to make *Ceviche*, which is one of the country's popular dishes. It is often marinated using lime juice, onions and red peppers and accompanied by chips. This is one of the meals you can find in most restaurants or from roadside food vendors.

The *tres leches,* referring to a three-milk cake, is the country's traditional dessert. Soaking the cake in cream, condensed milk and evaporated milk makes the dessert.

Fruit juices are always readily available given that the country has an abundance of tropical fruits. Some of the varieties you will find include: Sour Guava, referred to as *Cas*, is the Costa Rican native fruit; *Pina,* referring to pineapple; *Sandia,* referring to watermelon; *Mora,* referring to blackberry; and *frutas mixtas,* referring to a fruit punch. *Batido* is the equivalent of a smoothie and when ordering you will be asked *'con leche o agua'* meaning whether you prefer it with milk or water. *Horchata* is a traditional Costa Rican drink made from cinnamon and cornmeal.

Cerveceria de Costa Rica is the country's main brewery and brews 8 beer brands. Imperial beer is a favorite from the brewery, which is a conglomerate of the Florida Ice and Farm Company. The brewery has brewed Imperial since 1924 and they now distribute it to the Grand Cayman, U.S. and Australia. Bavaria (not the one from Holland) is also another favorite beer in the country alongside limejuice referred to as Rock Ice con limon and Heineken.

HOW TO SAVE MONEY ON FOOD IN COSTA RICA
One thing that you will appreciate in Costa Rica is that food is quite affordable. However, this is mostly the case when you are buying and cooking your own food. Eating out can be quite costly at times.

With a number of restaurants catering to the palates of international guests, the prices can get fairly steep. You can still get a decent low costs meal from a small authentic Costa Rican restaurant referred to as *sodas* and they come highly recommended if you aim at sampling authentic Costa Rican cuisines. Note that some of these eateries are very small and don't have table space. You will get a satisfying complete meal and dessert for $5 to $6.

Buy your fruits and vegetables from markets as opposed to supermarkets known as supermercado/mercado and they will be fairly cheap. Most towns have Saturday morning fairs referred to as ferias where you can buy varieties of produce affordably.

Chapter 6

WHAT TO DO IN COSTA RICA

One thing is certain when you are in Costa Rica; you will never be short of fun and exciting things to do.

COSTA RICA'S ATTRACTIONS

Costa Rica has a number of interesting historical and cultural monuments that you can visit. Some of them include:

Plaza De La Cultura

The Plaza of Culture located in San Jose hosts a number of interesting buildings and museums. It is also popular for the street vendors lining up the busy plaza. The National Theatre referred to as *Teatro Nacional* is found at the plaza as well as 2 city museums.

Arenal Volcano

The Arenal Volcano is one of Costa Rica's most active volcanos. The volcano still erupts occasionally and it has become a tourist attraction to view the smaller eruptions. Nearby are hot springs and white water rafting is popular in the region as well as repelling and hiking.

Cartago Ruins

Earthquakes twice destroyed the 18th century ruins of the Costa Rican colonial capital houses while they were being constructed. They still stand as historical monuments.

Corcovado National Park

If you are an outdoorsy kind of person a visit to the Corcovado National Park is highly recommended. Backpacking and hiking through one of the 13 ecosystems within the park, swimming along its beautiful coastal waters, playing in the roaring waterfall or simply laying on the golden sandy beaches are some of the activities this park offers. The mangroves and rainforest also provide the rare opportunity to see some of the country's endangered animals.

Monteverde Cloud Forest

At 4,600 feet above sea level, the Monteverde Cloud Forest is marked by lush greenery. The forest hosts 100 different mammal species and 400 insects and bird species. The forest is also home to 420 orchid species. The forest is ideal for zip lining, hiking as well as horseback riding. There are always tours to the forest and it is a worthwhile visit to enjoy the tranquil landscape.

Dominical

The beach town of Dominical is the perfect place to go surfing. If your ideal hang out plan is to lay on a hammock by the beach, then Dominical is the right place for you. It is one of the many low cost activities to do in Costa Rica.

Tortuguero

If you want to see endangered sea turtles, then the charming Caribbean town of Tortuguero is the place to be. The town also offers selections of wildlife to see including howler monkeys, green iguanas and sloths. If you are lucky, you might get to feast your eyes on the endangered manatees.

Llanos de Cortes

Who doesn't love to see a dramatic waterfall cascading down to a tranquil pond? A trip to the Llanos de Cortes is highly recommended if you also want to have a romantic picnic on the white sandy beaches against the backdrop of the waterfall.

Puerto Viejo

The Caribbean city of Puerto Viejo is popular with backpackers and young people in general. This is because it provides great beaches, with a party atmosphere and an ideal location to surf. There is always something going on every night and it has a distinct Rasta influence. However, for those looking for quieter places the city has selections of tranquil beach hotels.

ENTERTAINMENT IN COSTA RICA

Costa Rica is not on the global scale when it comes to creative arts and music. That doesn't mean that you can't enjoy some music in Costa Rica; in fact, the rich and diverse cultures add some spice to the music of the country. *Cumbia*, which is dance and music brought from Columbia and Africa, is one of the country's favorites.

Latin music like the *Bachata, Salsa* and *Meringue* are also quite popular in the country particularly with the older folk. *Reggeaeton*, that combines aspects of Jamaican dancehall and Reggae and Latin rhythms, is more popular with the younger generations.

The eastern side of the country has a predominant Afro-Caribbean population and Calypso, Reggae, Soca and Rumba music are popular in that area.

Costa Ricans enjoy listening to music from all around the world including Rock music, which is popular among the youth. Television stations from North America are accessible in Costa Rica giving them access to music channels like MTV and an influence of the pop culture.

Some of the country's major festivals that will keep you highly entertained include:

- In January all over the country are the *Fiestas de Palmares*. The fiestas include parades, carnivals, bingo and concerts.

- Every last week of February, the Sun Festival that promotes solar power use is held. The country also celebrates the Maya New Year with fire ceremonies every February 25th.

- Monterverde hosts a music festival running from February through March.

- Rey Curre, a village in the Bourca, hosts Fiestas of Diablos depicting fighting between the Spanish and Indians. It incorporates wooden masks, drum music and dancing, and fireworks in the evening.

- Every 2nd Sunday of March, the country celebrates Oxcart Drivers day referred to as the *Dia del Boyero*. Oxcarts, known as *carretas,* are a Costa Rican historical symbol because they were used to transport coffee beans to Puntarenas from the highlands and Central Valley.

- Playas Chiquita, which is located to the south of Puerto Viejo de Limon, hosts a Caribbean Music Festival running from March through April.

- The Guanacaste Day held to commemorate the annexation of Guanacaste with Costa Rica is celebrated every 25th of July. The celebrations feature folk dances, bull teasing and cattle shows.

- September 15th is the country's Independence Day and it celebrates the independence of Central American countries from the colonial rule of Spain. Paper lanterns made by children illuminate the streets as a nocturnal parade is conducted and the Freedom Torch is carried from Guatemala on to Costa Rica and on to the Central America colonial capital Cartago.

- The Festival of Corn, *Fiesta del Maiz*, is held on October 13th annually. It features costumes made using husks, silks of corn and grains.

- December is when a number of celebrations take place to usher in Christmas and the New Year. San Jose gets lit up with decorative lights all over and families compete to design nativity scenes, which goes on well through the 22nd of December. Expect to have a lot of coconut candy known as *melcochas*, eggnog known as *rompope*, boiled corn dough that is stuffed with diverse veggies and meat known as *tamales*, corn liquor known as *chichi*, and the equivalent of mashed potatoes and turkey which is rice with chicken referred to as *Arroz con Pollo*.

- A grand parade with a lot of music and decorative floats marks the commemoration of *Festejos Populares* on the 26th of December. It is held at Zapote, which is an amusement park/fair grounds in San Jose. New Year is marked like a huge community fiesta. Neighbors, who have forged strong bonds growing up together, have an open door policy and freely walk in each others homes joining in on parties.

NIGHTLIFE IN COSTA RICA

Costa Rica provides diverse options when it comes to nightlife activities.

The weekend (Fridays and Saturdays) is usually when people go clubbing in Costa Rica. However, ladies night or discount nights during the week are not uncommon and Costa Ricans simply love partying.

Some clubs/bars offer drinks at discounted rates before 9p.m., but 10 p.m. to 11 p.m. is when clubs really come into full swing. Closing time varies from one establishment to another, but usually closing time is between 2 a.m. to 4 a.m.

What people wear while out clubbing depends on the weather and most tourists are spotted with shorts, tank tops and flip-flops at clubs near the beach/costal towns. In the Central Valley, the weather tends to get colder at night and club patrons are known to dress more sophisticatedly. A nice dress, good pair of jeans and high heels for the ladies should do in most of the towns. There are some clubs that have dress codes and do not allow shorts, tank tops and hats.

Partying is a group affair in the country, with the exception of ladies night when most people go solo.

A noteworthy tip is that there is a distinct difference between a club and a nightclub in Costa Rica. A club equates to your normal dance club while a nightclub is often a strip club. If you are male and new to Costa Rica, asking for the best nightclub will elicit a couple of laughs.

Costa Ricans love dancing and everyone is welcome to bust their best moves on the dance floor. Some Merengue and Salsa knowledge will go a long way in keeping up with the locals on the dance floor. Costa Rican clubs often play Hip-hop, Merengue, Rock, Reggaeton, Salsa and Cumbia music.

Karaoke is quite popular as well and most towns have karaoke bars. San Jose hosts the best Karaoke clubs with both Spanish and English hits.

It is totally acceptable to ask a woman/man for a dance and Costa Ricans tend to be very direct about their intentions. Costa Rican women are very affectionate and direct as well. They also tend to be very flirtatious and a woman kissing a male colleague on the cheek is quite acceptable in Costa Rica. Costa Rican men talk animatedly with hand gestures and they do not shy away from staring at women. In general, most Costa Ricans still live at home with their families until marriage. Therefore, if the night does progress well couples looking for intimacy would go to the country's love motels referred to as *moteles*. Protection is easily available from grocery stores, bar/club bathrooms, pharmacies and *supermercados*. Some *moteles* also provide them at an extra fee.

HOW TO SAVE MONEY WHEN SIGHTSEEING IN COSTA RICA

With so much to do and a limited budget, you will definitely want to find creative ways to save money when sightseeing in Costa Rica.

One helpful tip is to travel around using the bus. If you don't have a lot of luggage and want to cover larger distances affordably, then Costa Rican buses are your best bet. For instance, taking a bus from San Jose to Manuel Antonia will cost you about $8, while a taxi trip will cost you up to $120. Also avoid tourist buses, which tend to be almost double the price of regular Costa Rican buses.

Most national parks charge an entrance fee of around $10, day trips/canopy tours $45 and two tank dives about $60. Always ask for student discounts or group discounts (if applicable). This will save you some money.

Most resorts /hostels will allow you to camp for about $5 and this will help you cut back on accommodation costs.

It goes without saying that you should know how to use the Costa Rican currency. Know how much any item in colones translates to your native currency; and most importantly, know how much you owe and how much you are owed in change. In general, $1 US translates to about 500 CRC. A helpful tip is to have a currency convertor app on your smartphone.

CHAPTER 7

MAKING MONEY IN COSTA RICA

The reason why most expats move to Costa Rica is to retire and live out the rest of their lives in this beautiful tropical country. However, not all who move to Costa Rica are at the pensionable age and some simply move to the country seeking adventure or a fresh start. For non-*pensionados*, you might want to know how to legally work in Costa Rica.

HOW TO GET A JOB IN COSTA RICA

Now contrary to what you might have heard - that you can pick up work as an English teacher in Costa Rica, this isn't entirely true. In order to legally get employed in Costa Rica you must be a citizen of the country or hold permanent residency status.

Unlike most third world countries where it is much easier for expats to get employment, Costa Rica has a very high literacy rate. This means that Costa Rican nationals are skilled enough to fill just about any job category that is available in the country. You could apply for a job listing and if you are deemed more skilled and qualified than a Costa Rican citizen, the employer may choose to apply for a one-year work permit on your behalf. However, this is quite a difficult and time-consuming process.

It is quite possible to get a job teaching English at a private school on a 2-year contract. As you can imagine this is quite a difficult opportunity to stumble upon and you must have at least a Master's degree to qualify for this job opportunity; an ESL certificate just won't cut it.

AVAILABLE WORK OPPORTUNITIES IN COSTA RICA

Jobs are available in Costa Rica, but what you should be careful about is working legally within the country. You can get a job where you have the requisite skillset and qualifications. Just remember that you must have permanent residency to legally gain such employment.

Another alternative to working in Costa Rica is to 'telecommute.' This basically means that you could still be working for a company back in your native country, but living in Costa Rica. This is legal and if you can get such a work opportunity by all means go ahead and make it work.

Working online could be the surest and easiest way to make money while living in Costa Rica. Whether through online work platforms, blogging or putting your skills to use; working online will get you the extra cash you need to keep you going in Costa Rica.

SALARIES/WAGES

If you do get a job legally in Costa Rica the first adjustment that you should make is on the compensation received. Generally, you can expect to earn about 15% less than what you would earn for the same job in the US/UK/Canada.

If you do gain permanent residency and can legally get long-term employment you might want to have a look at the Costa Rican minimum wage guidelines. Also, it goes without saying that you will need to be able to communicate in Spanish fluently.

VOLUNTEERING IN COSTA RICA

It is possible to work as a volunteer in Costa Rica. Most of these positions are teaching positions in schools through organizations like EVOLC, WorldTeach and Projects Aboard. These volunteer opportunities last from a week up to a year. Most are unpaid, but your accommodation is provided.

CHAPTER 8

EDUCATION IN COSTA RICA

It is natural to want to know more about formal education programs available in Costa Rica, whether for yourself or a loved one that you will travel with. Maybe you are going to Costa Rica to attend school. As mentioned, the Costa Rican government invested a lot of resources in education after the abolishment of the army. Therefore, the education system is very structured with private and public schools including language schools.

THE SCHOOL SYSTEM

Costa Rica made education mandatory and free for all citizens in 1869. Since then, the country has put 30% of the national budget towards primary and secondary school education.

Public elementary schools as well as high schools are found in every town/city. Students wear uniforms in school. Students go through 6 years of public elementary school and then 5 to 6 years of high school education. The first 3 years in high school provides general education to students and the remaining 2 to 3 years provide specialized training. Students then undertake sciences or arts courses to obtain the *Bachillereto Diploma* accredited by the Ministry of Education in Costa Rica.

Private schools are found throughout the country offering classes in diverse languages and some follow the U.S. curriculum. The private schools offer U.S. High School Diplomas accredited by SACS (Southern Association of Colleges and Schools) and the International Baccalaureate Diploma that is accredited by the Switzerland IBO.

The country also provides both public and private colleges/universities. The tuition fees are generally about half that of

U.S. based universities. Courses are taught in Spanish, but there are courses that are taught in English. Most private universities including the Universidad Latinoamericana de Ciencia y Tecnologia and Universidad de Iberoamerica provide majors that are taught in English. Students also have the opportunity to spend some time abroad and most graduate with little or no debt in student loans.

The University of Costa Rica offers over 100 undergraduate as well as postgraduate degrees and is ranked highest amongst the country's public universities.

If you are a U.S. based university student you could look into a study abroad opportunity to Costa Rica. Different schools provide these opportunities for different durations going from one semester or a full year. However, you should know that you would be in charge of several arrangements including admission tests and student loans. You will also have to get a student visa if you are looking into being in Costa Rica for more than 3 months.

PAYING FOR SCHOOL

At the University of Costa Rica tuition is about $80 per credit and $140 per credit for undergraduates and postgraduates, respectively. On average, 17 credits is the undergraduate course load per semester meaning that tuition per year is around $2,800. Miscellaneous fees cost about $100 annually and living expenses are about $500 to $1,500 monthly. Graduate students with about 14 credits per semester will end up paying about $4,000 annually inclusive of living costs. The Universidad Estatal a Distancia (Distance Learning University) have similar credit costs.

There are scholarship opportunities as well as financial aid available for students in Costa Rica. The application process is similar to how you would apply for student loans or scholarships in the United States or other parts of the world.

SPANISH LANGUAGE SCHOOLS IN COSTA RICA

It goes without saying that you will need to learn Spanish to thrive in Costa Rica. Spanish is the national language spoken in the country and most of the websites related to the country are in Spanish. You could opt to join one of the many Spanish schools in Costa Rica to learn the language.

An advantage of joining one of the Spanish schools in Costa Rica is that you will be able to get a resource of information about the country. The schools also provide Homestay accommodation with shared rooms and single room options. This also allows you to possibly meet people from your native country on a similar Costa Rican adventure; it is always helpful to have a fellow expat to turn to in any foreign country.

Language schools are a great place to start learning the basics of Spanish and you can then immerse yourself into the Costa Rican culture to gain a deeper understanding of the language. Tuition at these schools cost anywhere from $600 to $1,200 for 2 weeks of lessons including accommodation, meals (full board, half board and in some cases no meals) and school administrative fees.

In most places including the capital, big hotels, and businesses you will find Costa Ricans who speak in English. Always ask to hold a conversation in Spanish to help you practice as well as learn the language further.

Chapter 9

SHIPPING AND MAIL SERVICE IN COSTA RICA

Once you are settled in Costa Rica and have permanent residency status you may want to import a few comforts from home. This could be furniture, artwork or trinkets that you have been collecting over the years as well as a myriad of your personal possessions. So how would you go about getting them to Costa Rica?

MAIL

The Post Office in Costa Rica is referred to as *Correos de Costa Rica*. One of the first living abroad adjustments you have to make is that most places don't have reliable home mail delivery systems. If you wish to receive snail mail you will have to get a post office box known as an *apartado*. This will cost you about $8 to $12 annually, but you should know that it would take up to one year to get a mailbox once you apply for one.

You would have to visit the post office to regularly check whether you have received mail. It takes anywhere from 3 to 4 weeks to receive snail mail from the U.S.

Mail courier services are also available in Costa Rica. Several services will provide two addresses for you to receive snail mail and packages from online shopping. Setting up an account is quite easy and most services have English speaking staff, but their websites are often in Spanish. You will have to pay a refundable deposit to set up such a service and it is about $15 monthly. Worth noting is that some of these services keep records of your purchases, because legally you can ship in $500 worth of merchandise duty free every 6 month period. This is actually a very handy way of saving on import duties.

For important utility bills or credit card bills, you are best served by receiving bills to your designated email address. With up to 4 week waits to receive snail mail, you could end up paying a lot in late payment fees. This is why online banking also comes in handy to keep up with your U.S. or native country bill payments when you are in Costa Rica.

MODES OF SHIPPING

To make your move as orderly and painless as possible, enlist the services of a professional mover. In this case, you would have two movers; one helping you in your native country and the other in Costa Rica. Work with your Costa Rican mover every step of the way to ensure that all the items you want brought to you are listed on the manifest and that they all get to you.

A popular mode of shipping is through ports, but you can also have your items flown in or if you are moving from a nearby country have them transported by road. Ports are the most common mode of shipping used by people from the U.S.

One thing you should know is that it is very expensive to ship items to Costa Rica. Even old, used items will incur a tax of anywhere from 40% to 90% of the cost of the item. After adding shipping costs, you are paying heftily for the luxury of having your items shipped to the country.

Shipping overland, though not available or a popular choice, is also available. There are trucking companies that offer overland shipping services via Mexico to Central America. There is always risk of delays at the borders and theft, which is the reason why this method is not as popular.

OTHER METHODS TO BRING ITEMS TO COSTA RICA

So if you simply must have some of your items with you and can't afford the hefty shipping costs, consider having friends or family bring them in. Tourists often get waved through customs without having their luggage checked. However, this might not always be the case so it is not a full proof way to bring your items in. This will work mostly for smaller items that you feel like you simply must have with you.

Tourism is a major contributor to the Costa Rican economy; therefore, the Costa Rican government is very accommodating in certain cases. For instance, they understand that tourists need sports equipment, stereos, musical instruments, bicycles and personal computers to make the most out of their Costa Rican experience. Personal items, in general, will be allowed through customs as long as the items are not taken into the country for resale purposes. The number of items brought in also has to be reasonable and in most cases airlines allow 2 pieces of luggage with each not exceeding 50 pounds. If you have excess luggage you will be required to fill out a declaration form.

Some airlines will allow you to book air cargo and one of the highly recommended ones is American Airline Cargo. This is for small amounts less than 500 pounds in weight. The cost is often based on total weight or dimension of boxes being shipped, but generally it is about $1 per pound. Standard and express freight options are offered, and with standard freight it takes anywhere from 2 to 5 days to get your cargo in Costa Rica. This is of course subject to space-availability on airlines.

HOW TO SAVE ON SHIPPING COSTS

You will be charged based on a per hundredweight basis, which can be quite costly depending on the weight and how much you have to ship. It is not uncommon to pay $10,000 or more to ship your items to Costa Rica. Therefore, it makes sense to look for ways to save on moving costs when shipping your items to Costa Rica.

The surest way to save on shipping costs is to only ship what you absolutely need. Furniture, for instance, is not a priority when it comes to items you want to ship. This is because furniture is very affordable in Costa Rica. It might make sense to dispose of your old furniture and buy new furniture once you are in Costa Rica. Electronics are generally more expensive in Costa Rica so shipping in your must-have electronics is probably a good idea.

Also, it is very important to get a good moving/shipping agent. They may end up saving you some money in terms of import duties. You should note that you would have to pay import duties in order to collect your items from the Costa Rican port.

One ill-advised tip to save on shipping costs is not to insure the items you are shipping in. By doing this, you will not have declared the cost of each item, and hence, you won't have to pay tax or pay marginally lower taxes on the items you ship in. This is a definite gamble should your items incur damages during transit.

Chapter 10

GETTING MARRIED IN COSTA RICA

Finding a companion is a major milestone in life. If this stage of life has alluded you thus far or you've experienced it and it didn't quite workout; who knows, your better half might just be waiting for you in Costa Rica. Let's say you meet someone, start up a relationship, and finally you are ready to take your relationship to the next step – marriage. How do you go about getting married in Costa Rica?

MARRIAGE LAWS IN COSTA RICA

Costa Rica allows foreign nationals to get married in the country (whether to Costa Rican nationals or otherwise). To get married legally in Costa Rica, you will need to have the following documents:

- Original birth certificates (yours and your wife/husband to be)
- Divorce certificates (for those who have been married before)
- An affidavit declaring your single status
- Police record
- Valid passport

These documents must be presented to a Costa Rican Embassy within your country of origin before going to Costa Rica to proceed with the marriage. Stamps, referred to as *timbres*, will be attached to the documents and they will be returned to you. The costs associated with this is about $40 for each document.

Most people simply have civil ceremonies officiated by local lawyers. Thereafter, the lawyer is tasked with recording the marriage under the Costa Rica National Registry. An official marriage certificate is then issued, which is valid outside the country as well, but has to be translated to English so that it is recognized legally in Canada or the U.S. The process takes anywhere from 4 to 6 weeks.

It is important to consult with a marriage attorney in Costa Rica for updated and comprehensive legal requirements.

WEDDING VENUES IN COSTA RICA

You will have a myriad of options when it comes to selecting a Costa Rican wedding venue. From Pristine beaches, city locations and Tropical Forests; Costa Rica offers a wide range of wedding venue options.

One of the things that you will love about getting married in Costa Rica is combining your dream wedding with a family/friends vacation as well as your honeymoon. Some of the popular wedding venues in Costa Rica include:

Beach Venues

The Northern and Central Pacific offer unique beach wedding venues. The Northern Pacific offers beautiful landscapes splattered with hills, gulfs and bays, cliffs and forests. The panoramic routes and beautiful golden and white sandy beaches with clear blue waters make it a popular beach wedding destination.

The Central Pacific hosts the Manuel Antonio National Park, which is a world-acclaimed rainforest reserve and home to indigenous wildlife. It also has vast white sandy beaches and lush jungles. Some of the venues to look up include:

- Arenas del Mar
- Hotel Punta Islita
- Four Seasons Costa Rica

- Gala Boutique Hotel
- Tango Mar Beach hotel, Golf Resort and Spa
- Hotel Villa Caletas

San Jose Central Valley Venues

The Central Valley hosts the Juan Santamaria International Airport (SJO), making it another easily accessible wedding destination. The Central Valley also hosts coffee plantations, volcanoes, handcraft shops, and museums and theatres. Some of the venues to look up include:

- Alta Hotel
- Costa Rica Marriott
- Finca Rosa Blanco Hotel and Spa
- El Silencio Lodge and Spa
- Xandari Resort and Spa

Countryside Venues

The countryside provides vast beautiful landscapes with fields of crops, forests, hot springs, rivers and lagoons. The countryside provides tranquil and romantic wedding getaways. Some of the venues to look up include:

- Arenal Nayara Hote, Spa and Gardens
- Villa Blanca Cloud Forest Hotel
- Arenal Kioro Hotel Suites and Spa
- The Springs Resort and Spa

PLANNING A WEDDING IN COSTA RICA

Planning a wedding in Costa Rica isn't really different from planning a wedding anywhere else. You could choose to go it alone or enlist the services of a wedding planner. There are very good wedding planners in Costa Rica and the best way to find one is through referrals from online platforms.

Maintain constant communication with your wedding planner, if you do choose to go with one, to make sure that everything is on track. Note that you will require two witnesses (non-family) present during the ceremony and your wedding planner should be able to arrange this on your behalf.

In the case of having your friends and family fly down for the wedding, let them know well in advance. Flying, in general, can be quite costly and a little planning time is needed. Also, choose venues as well as accommodation with your friends and family in mind. Not everyone will be able to afford accommodation at luxurious and expensive resorts. Also, pick dates that are favorable in terms of flight costs to allow your loved ones to fly in affordably.

Pay attention to the weather, particularly if your wedding will be at the beach or in the mountainous regions. Unexpected rains are a wedding nightmare around the globe and you definitely don't want them ruining your big day.

Last but not least, give the planning process your all and above all enjoy it. A wedding is a symbol of a union that you are forging with a person you love and it is in every sense a celebration of that union.

HOW TO SAVE ON WEDDING COSTS IN COSTA RICA

The average cost of a wedding in the U.S. is $30,000, but one thing is for sure that it will be marginally less in Costa Rica. However, if you intend to have friends and family fly down to the beautiful paradise for your magical wedding you will want to make the most out of your wedding budget.

Go for wedding packages because they will save you a lot of money. For instance, on average, a $5,000 budget can cover venue charges, flowers, the officiant, dinner and drinks for about 50 guests and a cake. Your guest number and the general details of your wedding determine the general cost.

As unromantic as they appear to be, another way to save on wedding costs would be to have a simple civil wedding. If you are cash strapped this would do just fine and what matters most is legally officiating a marriage with the person you love.

About the Author

Melissa Nicole Johnson is an American expat raised in Atlanta, Georgia. In her spare time Melissa enjoys traveling, writing books, and educating people about traveling and living outside the United States.

OTHER BOOKS FEATURED BY INSPIRED WORD PUBLISHERS

You can find other titles and books by our authors available on Amazon.

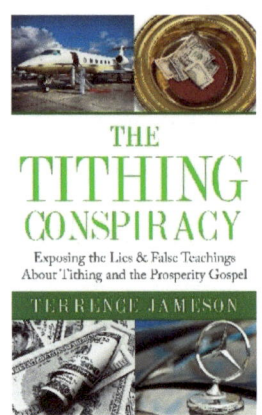

ONE LAST THING

If you enjoyed this book or found it useful I would be grateful if you would post a short review on Amazon. Your support really does make a difference and inspires others to take action and also learn how this book has helped you.

Thank you again for your support.

www.ingramcontent.com/pod-product-compliance
Lightning Source LLC
Chambersburg PA
CBHW042217050426
42453CB00001BA/1